# Starter Guide to
# Among Us

by Josh Gregory

CHERRY LAKE PRESS
Ann Arbor, Michigan

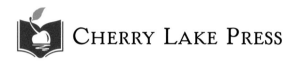

Published in the United States of America by Cherry Lake Publishing
Ann Arbor, Michigan
www.cherrylakepublishing.com

Reading Adviser: Beth Walker Gambro, MS, Ed., Reading Consultant, Yorkville, IL

Photo Credits: Images by Josh Gregory

**Cherry Lake Press** is an imprint of Cherry Lake Publishing Group.

Library of Congress Cataloging-in-Publication Data has been filed and is available at catalog.loc.gov

Printed in the United States of America by
Corporate Graphics

Note from the Publisher: Websites change regularly, and their future contents are outside of our control. Supervise children when conducting any recommended online searches for extended learning opportunities.

# Contents

# A Surprise Hit

Even though its graphics are plain, *Among Us* is fun to play. The setting of the game is outer space.

*Among Us* came out in 2018. It was created by a small company called Innersloth. Innersloth's **developers** had a small **budget**. So they used simple **graphics**. But the game's idea was good. More and more people started playing. Soon after, *Among Us* shot to fame. Today, it's enjoyed by millions of players!

# The Idea

Enrique was not An Impostor.

The goal of *Among Us* is to find the enemy, or Impostor, in a group of players.

The idea for *Among Us* came from earlier mystery games. Games like this are known as social **deduction** games. The idea is simple. Players must figure out which other players are secret enemies. And the enemy players must lie, or **bluff**, to keep from being discovered.

# Jumping In

You can play *Among Us* on just about any computer or handheld device.

When you open the game's main menu, you'll find a few options. Choose what's best for you. An *Among Us* match can have anywhere from 4 to 15 players. Of those, 1 to 3 will be chosen at **random** to be Impostors. The rest of the players are Crewmates. Crewmates don't know who's an Impostor. Yet Impostors know who the other Impostors are.

## Famous Fans

Many well-known influencers play *Among Us*. Even a member of the U.S. Congress, Alexandria Ocasio-Cortez, joined the fun!

# Crewmates

Crewmates will know how many Impostors are in a match.

As a Crewmate, you must complete tasks. The list of tasks appears in the upper left corner of the screen. Each task takes place in a different room. You must also complete mini-games and puzzles. As you play, try to figure out who is an Impostor. Impostors look just like Crewmates. So finding them is tricky.

## Map

Click on the map icon in the upper right of your screen. It will show you where you need to go to complete the tasks.

# How to Win?

Custom Settings
Map: The Skeld
# Impostors: 2
Confirm Ejects: On
# Emergency Meetings
Anonymous Votes: Off
Emergency Cooldown: 20s
Discussion Time: 30s
Voting Time: 45s
Player Speed: 2x
Crewmate Vision: 5x
Impostor Vision: 2.5x
Kill Cooldown: 15s
Kill Distance: Long
Task Bar Updates: Always
Visual Tasks: On
# Common Tasks: 2
# Long Tasks: 2
# Short Tasks: 2

Ping: 50 ms

Color   Hat   Pet   Skin   Game

PUBLIC   Code
JHIBKF   7/10

Your character's appearance is just for fun! It doesn't give you any advantages in the game.

Crewmates have two ways to win. They complete their tasks or discover all the Impostors. Impostors can win if they **eliminate** all Crewmates. They can also **sabotage** certain systems to win. When an Impostor attacks a Crewmate, the Crewmate falls to the ground. The game pauses. Then the players can call a meeting.

## Your Appearance

Players pick their character's appearance. They can choose from different colors, hats, and pets. Players can also purchase more options. But don't buy anything without talking to an adult!

# Meetings

Winning *Among Us* requires a lot of skills. You must figure out when someone is lying!

At the meeting, players can discuss who the **culprit** is. Many players enjoy this part of the game. Impostors can bluff. They pretend to be Crewmates. Meanwhile, Crewmates try to identify the Impostors. Then all the players vote on who the Impostor is. The player who loses the vote is eliminated from the game. Impostors may lie to eliminate Crewmates. Be careful who you believe!

# Teamwork

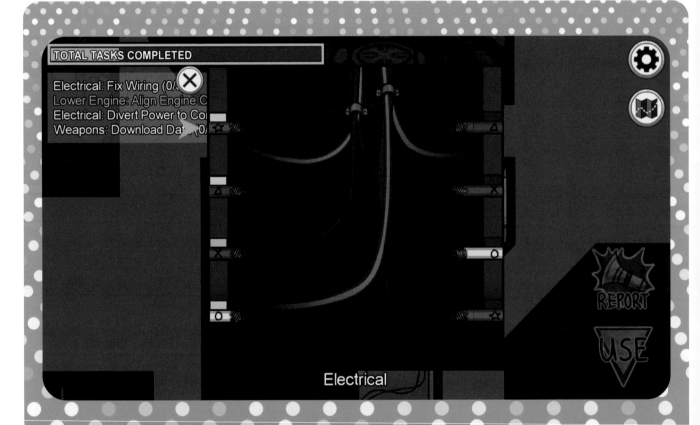

TOTAL TASKS COMPLETED

Electrical: Fix Wiring (0/
Lower Engine: Align Engine C
Electrical: Divert Power to Co
Weapons: Download Da (0/

Electrical

There are several levels to *Among Us*. Each has a different layout and tasks. In this task, you must connect matching wires.

Work with your Crewmates to identify Impostors and finish tasks. There are easy and hard tasks. Some require many steps to complete. As you work, keep an eye out for Impostors. They can't perform tasks. Although they often pretend to. Try to spot one. Also, if you find a player attacking a Crewmember, it's an Impostor!

## Freeplay

Want to practice tasks? Select "Freeplay" from the main menu. Then you can try your hand at different tasks with no other players.

# Extra Skills

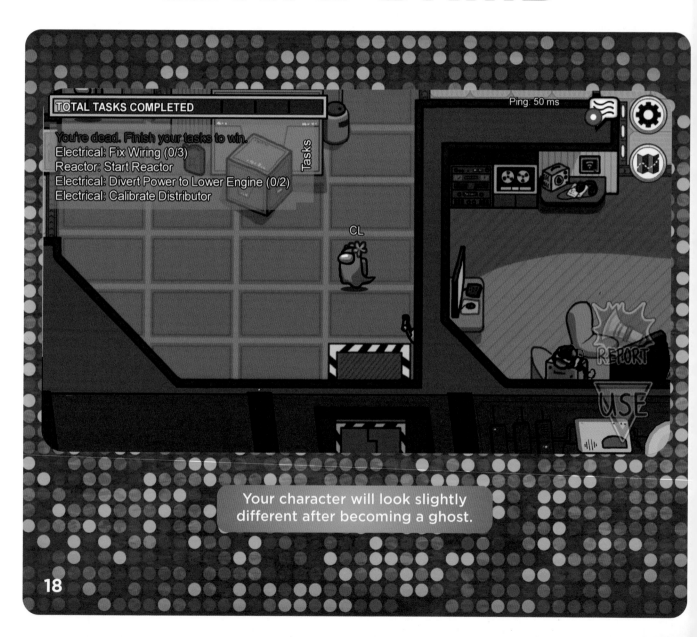

TOTAL TASKS COMPLETED

You're dead. Finish your tasks to win.
Electrical: Fix Wiring (0/3)
Reactor: Start Reactor
Electrical: Divert Power to Lower Engine (0/2)
Electrical: Calibrate Distributor

Tasks

CL

Ping: 50 ms

REPORT

USE

Your character will look slightly different after becoming a ghost.

If you think you've found an Impostor, call a meeting. Explain what you saw. Make sure you have **evidence**. If you are an Impostor, your goal is to blend in. Watch out for cameras. Crewmates can check cameras to spy on Impostors. When the time is right, attack a Crewmember. But make sure you don't get caught!

## Ghosts

If an Impostor knocks you out, you'll become a ghost. Ghosts can only talk to other ghosts. They can't call meetings. Yet they can still complete tasks and help their team!

# What's Next?

When you see this screen, you know something big has happened!

It won't take long for you to get a feel for *Among Us*. Still, every match has surprises. Study how other people play. Seeing how players bluff is a big part of the game. Don't worry if you don't win every round. Just focus on having fun! You'll be a great player in no time.

# GLOSSARY

**bluff** (BLUHF) to make a false claim to trick someone; to pretend

**budget** (BUHJ-it) the amount of money available for something

**culprit** (KUHL-prit) someone who is guilty of something

**deduction** (deh-DUK-shuhn) the process of figuring something out through careful reasoning

**developers** (dih-VEL-uh-purz) people who make video games or other computer programs

**eliminate** (ih-LIM-uh-neyt) to remove or get rid of something

**evidence** (EV-uh-duhnss) information and facts that help prove something

**graphics** (GRAF-iks) images made by a computer

**random** (RAN-duhm) done without a conscious decision

**sabotage** (SAB-uh-tahj) to deliberately cause something to malfunction

# FIND OUT MORE

## BOOKS

Gregory, Josh. *Among Us: Beginner's Guide*. Ann Arbor, MI: Cherry Lake Publishing, 2022.

Loh-Hagan, Virginia. *Video Games*. Ann Arbor, MI: Cherry Lake Publishing, 2021.

Powell, Marie. *Asking Questions About Video Games*. Ann Arbor, MI: Cherry Lake Publishing, 2016.

## WEBSITES

With an adult, learn more online with these suggested searches:

**Among Us**
Check out Innersloth's official *Among Us* site for the latest updates on the game's development.

**Among Us Wiki**
This fan-created site is packed with info about every detail of *Among Us*.

# INDEX

# ABOUT THE AUTHOR

**Josh Gregory** is the author of more than 200 books for kids. He has written about everything from animals to technology to history. A graduate of the University of Missouri–Columbia, he currently lives in Chicago, Illinois.